Horst Goetzmann · Horst Wöbbeking
Schleswig-Holstein

Ein Foto-Kunst-Band
mit englischer Übersetzung von Priscilla Metscher

© 1990 by Verlag Atelier im Bauernhaus
D-2802 Fischerhude
Layout: Wolf-Dietmar Stock
Satz: Fotosatz Wahlers, Langwedel
Lithos: Rüdiger & Doepner, Bremen
Druck: Girzig & Gottschalk, Bremen
ISBN 3-88 132 157-8

Schleswig-Holstein
fotografiert von Horst Wöbbeking
mit Texten von Horst Goetzmann

4

SCHLESWIG-HOLSTEIN

meerumschlungen, deutscher Sitte hohe Wacht ..." dichtete Matthias
Fr. Chemnitz aus Barmstedt und sein Text wurde 1844 zum ersten Mal als
Schleswig-Holstein-Lied gesungen. Von Nord- und Ostsee umspült war dieses
Gebiet denn auch jahrhundertelang der nördlichste Teil deutschen Landes.
Seit Karl der Große 798 den westlichen Landesteil in sein fränkisches Reich
eingliederte und die Schauenburger Grafen im 12. Jh. die Herrschaft der Slawen
brachen, waren die Landesteile Schleswig und Holstein jeweils Vorposten
gegen die Dänen im Norden und die Wenden im Osten.
Im Vertrag von Ripen hieß es dann 1460, daß Schleswig (dänisches Lehen) und
Holstein (deutsches Lehen) „bliven tosamende ewig ungedeelt" [auf ewig
ungeteilt zusammen bleiben sollen]. Und so ist es denn bis heute, wenn man
einmal von der Sonderstellung Lübecks absieht, das – 1159 gegründet –
von Kaiser Friedrich II. 1226 zur freien Reichsstadt erklärt wurde und dies bis
1937 blieb.
Im Gegensatz zur recht komplizierten politischen Geschichte des Landes läßt
sich die Landschaft sehr klar gliedern:
– Im Westen die Nordsee mit 536 km Küste, mit Inseln, Halligen und dem Watt,
das im steten Wechsel von 12 Stunden bei Ebbe sichtbar wird und bei Flut
verschwindet. Gegen die Unberechenbarkeit der Natur mit ihren (Sturm-)Fluten
haben sich die Menschen durch Deiche geschützt.
– Landeinwärts, hinter den Deichen, liegen die fruchtbaren Marschen
(Niederungen), die sich durch abgelagerten Schlick und Schlamm gebildet
haben, den die Flut herangespült hat. Mit Hilfe eingedeichter Flachwasserareale
(Kooge, Polder) versucht der Mensch, indem er das Wasser ablaufen und
verdunsten läßt, wieder festes Land zu gewinnen.
– Was hier für die Nordsee gesagt wurde, gilt im gleichen Maße auch im
Süden des Landes für die Uferbereiche der Elbe, die durch ihre eigene
Wasserzufuhr und durch den Tidenhub (die unterschiedlichen Wasserstände
zwischen Ebbe und Flut) die Menschen gelehrt hat, sich auch im Landesinnern
vor den Hochwassern zu schützen.

– An die See- und Flußmarschen schließt sich mit Feldern, Knicks und Seen das eigentliche Binnenland an; es ist geprägt durch die Moränenlandschaft der Hohen und Niederen Geest und durch das östliche Hügelland im Bereich der Ostsee. Während der Eiszeiten haben gewaltige, aus Skandinavien kommende Gletscher große Massen von Geröll, Kies und Geschiebe vor sich hergeschoben und nach dem Abtauen hier abgelagert. Diese Moränen bestimmen mit Kies und Gestein die hügeligen Bodenformen der Geest (ödes Land) und mit Sand und Geschiebe den fruchtbaren östlichen Landesteil. Die unregelmäßigen Ablagerungen sind auch verantwortlich dafür, daß die Schmelzwasser der Gletscher nicht in jedem Fall abfließen konnten: 300 Binnenseen (140 in der „Holsteinischen Schweiz") sind charakteristisch für die schleswig-holsteinische Landschaft.

– Da, wo die Wassermassen vor rund 15 000 Jahren ins Ostseebecken gelangen konnten, entstanden an der 384 km langen Ostseeküste tief ins Land geschnittene Förden (von Flensburg bis Kiel) und Buchten (Lübeck), heute ein reizvoller, abwechslungsreicher Gegensatz zu der Landschaft und dem Klima an der Nordsee.

Verständlicherweise hat nicht nur die Natur das Land geprägt. Älteste menschliche Funde weisen hier 7 500 Jahre zurück. Heute noch sichtbare Zeugen menschlicher Besiedlung sind die zahlreichen Stein- und Hügelgräber aus den Jahrtausenden vor unserer Zeitrechnung. Neuzeitlich sind es die Kirchenbauten in Flensburg, Schleswig und Lübeck, die auf eine rund 800jährige Kulturgeschichte verweisen. Dank ihrer Bedeutung als „Königin der Hanse" im Mittelalter sind besonders in der Hansestadt Lübeck Zeugen aller folgenden Jahrhunderte reichlich zu finden, die geprägt sind durch heimisches Handwerk, Kunst und internationalen Handel. Diese Brückenfunktion zwischen Nord und Süd und West und Ost hat das ganze Land und seine Menschen seit jeher geformt. Aus ihr entwickelte sich der besondere Reiz Schleswig-Holsteins, „meerumschlungen ... up ewig ungedeelt."

Mit diesem Buch haben wir für Sie eine Fahrtroute arrangiert, um dieses Land in seiner Vielfalt zu entdecken. Wir wünschen Ihnen eine genußvolle optische Reise!

"Schleswig-Holstein, sea-embraced, sublime guardian of German custom …"
the poet Matthias Fr. Chemnitz from Barmstedt wrote and his text was sung for
the first time in 1844 as the Schleswig-Holstein-song. Washed by the North Sea
and the Baltic, for centuries this has been the most northerly part of German
territory. Ever since Charles the Great incorporated the western part into his
Frankish Empire in 798 and the Schauenburg earls broke the rule of the Slavs
in the 12th century the regions of Schleswig and Holstein have alternately been
outposts against the Danes in the North and the Wends in the East.
In the Treaty of Ripen in 1460 it was stated that Schleswig (Danish Lehen) and
Holstein (German Lehen) "should remain together undivided for ever." And so
it has been to the present day, exept for the special status of Lübeck which –
founded in 1159 by Emperor Frederick II – was declared a free imperial city in
1226 and remained so until 1937. In contrast to the rather complicated political
history of the region the countryside can be very clearly structured:
– In the west the North Sea with 536 km of coast with islands, holms ('Hallige')
and mud flats, which in a continuous alternation of 12 hours become visible at
low tide and disappear at high tide. The people have protected themselves
against the unpredictability of nature with its floods by building dykes.
– Inland, behind the dykes are the fertile marshes (marsh lowlands), which
have been formed by deposited silt and mud washed up by the high tide. With
the aid of shallow water areas (Kooge, Polder) people have tried to regain land
by letting the water drain away and evaporate.
– What has been said here about the North Sea is true also of the south of
the region on the banks of the Elbe: through its own influx of water and its
'tidal heave' (the different water levels between high and low tide) people
inland have too been taught to protect themselves against floods.
– The actual interior is connected to the sea and river marshes by fields, quick
- set - hedges ('Knicks') and lakes: it is stamped by the moraine landscape of
the 'high and low geest' and by the eastern hilly countryside near the Baltic.
During the Ice Age huge glaciers coming from Scandinavia pushed great masses
of scree, gravel and boulders before them, and having melted deposited them
here. These moraines with gravel and rocks determine the hilly earth shapes of

the geest (waste land) and with sand and boulders the fertile eastern part of the region. Because of the irregular deposits the melted water of the glaciers could not always flow away: 300 inland lakes (140 in 'Holstein Switzerland', Holsteinischer Schweiz) are charateristic of Schleswig-Holstein's countryside. – Where the water masses did succeed in reaching the Baltic basin about 15,000 years ago, fjords came into existence (from Flensburg to Kiel), cutting deep into the land along the Baltic coast, 384 km. long and bays (Lübeck); today offering a contrast of charm and variety to the countryside and climate of the North Sea.

Understandably not only nature has left its stamp on the land. The oldest traces of human civilisation found point back to a period of 7,500 years ago. Today still visible witnesses of human settlements are the many cairns and tumuli of many thousand years BC. In modern times it is the church buildings in Flensburg, Schleswig and Lübeck which refer back to an 800 year old cultural history. Thanks to her importance as "Queen of the Hanse" in the Middle Ages the Hanseatic city of Lübeck has numerous buildings which are witnesses to all the ensuing centuries. They have been stamped by native craftsmanship, art and international trade. This bridging function between the North and South, West and East has shaped the whole region and its people from time immemorial. Out of this the special charm of Schleswig-Holstein has developed "sea-embraced … undivided for ever."

With this book we have put together a travel route which shows this region in all its variety. We wish you an enjoyable visual journey!

Zwischen Lauenburg im Osten und dem Wattenmeer im Westen ist die aus der Tschechoslowakei kommende Elbe für über 150 km Schleswig-Holsteins Grenzfluß nach Süden. Nur das Land Hamburg unterbricht diese direkte Nachbarschaft zum gegenüberliegenden Niedersachsen.

Between Lauenburg in the East and the mud flats in the West the Elbe originating in Czechoslovakia is the river forming Schleswig-Holstein's border southwards for over 150 km. Only the 'Land' of Hamburg interrupts this direct proximity to Lower Saxony (Niedersachsen) on the other side.

Eine „malerische Schifferstadt am großen Strom" kann sich Lauenburg zu Recht nennen. Mit den Fachwerkhäusern entlang der Uferstraße und in den Hohlwegen am Elbhang ist viel kleinstädtisches Flair in der über 700 Jahre alten Unterstadt erhalten geblieben.

Lauenburg has every right to call itself a "pictuesque bargeman's town beside the big river." With its half-timbered houses along the embankment and in the hollowed-out paths at the Elbe much small town charm still exists in the 700 year-old lower town.

Das um 1795 gebaute Gutshaus Emkendorf gilt als Musterbeispiel klassi-
zistischer Herrenhauskultur. Durch Julia Gräfin von Reventlow und ihren Kreis
(Klopstock, Lavater, M. Claudius) wurde Emkendorf zum kulturellen
und geistigen Mittelpunkt im frühen 19. Jahrhundert.

Emkendorf manor, built in 1795 is a model of classical manorial culture. The
Countess Julia von Reventlow and her circle (Klopstock, Lavater, M. Claudius)
made Emkendorf a cultural and intellectual centre in the early 19th century.

Das Herrenhaus Wotersen wurde in der 1. Hälfte des 18. Jahrhunderts für den Kriegsrat Engelke von Bernstorff als spätbarocke, dreiflügelige Anlage mit dem Ehrenhof und ausgedehntem Park gebaut. Bekannt geworden ist das Anwesen als „Schloß Guldenburg" der ZDF-Fernsehserie.

Wotersen manor was built in the first half of the 18th century for Engelke von Bernstorff, military councillor. It is a late Baroque construction with three wings, a courtyard and extensive park. It is known as "Castle Guldenburg" in the ZDF-TV series.

Der Typ des niederdeutschen Hallenhauses ist besonders im südlichen Landesteil, wie hier in Husberg/Kreis Plön, anzutreffen. Hier lebten Mensch und Tier unter einem Dach, das – reet- oder strohgedeckt – auch noch die Vorräte und das Futter aufnahm.

This type of Low German 'Hallenhaus' is to be found especially in the southern part of the region as here in Husberg, rural district of Plön. Here people and animals lived under the one thatched roof which housed provisions and animal fodder.

Die evangelische Vicelin-Kirche in Neumünster wurde 1828/34 als rechteckige, klassizistische Saalkirche vom dänischen Baudirektor Hansen errichtet. Ihren Namen hat sie von Vicelin, dem „Apostel der Wenden", dessen Chorherrschaft hier 1163 geweiht wurde.

The Protestant Vicelin-Church in Neumünster was erected by Hansen the Danish builder in 1828/34 as a rectangular, classical church. Its name comes from Vicelin, the 'Apostel of Wenden' whose canon foundation was consecrated here in 1163.

Till Eulenspiegel verspricht Glück – wie sein vom Anfassen blanker Daumen und Fuß am Möllner Markt beweisen. Die Überlieferungen des 1350 in Mölln verstorbenen Schelms locken jährlich viele Tausend Besucher in den Kneipp-Kurort an der „Alten Salzstraße".

Till Eulenspiegel promises good fortune as his thumb and foot in Mölln market square indicate, shiny from touching. The traditions connected with this rogue who died in Mölln in 1350 attract many thousands of visitors yearly to the 'Kneipp' – health resort on the 'Old Saltway' (Alter Salzstraße).

Daneben bietet das über 800 Jahre alte Mölln viel mittelalterliche Atmosphäre mit der alles überragenden, gotischen Nikolaikirche und zahlreiche Erholungs- und Freizeitmöglichkeiten inmitten des wasser- und waldreichen Naturparks „Lauenburgische Seen".

In addition 800 year-old Mölln offers a mediaeval atmosphere with its Gothic Nikolai Church rising above everything and its many possibilities for recreation and leisure in the national park of the 'Lauenburg Lakes', rich in water and forest.

Zwölf km lang und zwei km breit: der Ratzeburger See ist ein ideales Wassersportrevier, nicht nur für Segler. Passagierdampfer bringen „Seereisende" vom südlichen Ratzeburg zum nördlichen Rothenhusen und – über die romantische Wakenitz – in die Hansestadt Lübeck.

12 km long and 2 km broad, Lake Ratzeburg is ideal for water sport, not only for sailing. Passenger steamers bring 'travellers' from Southern Ratzeburg to Northern Rothenhusen and – across the romantic Wakenitz – to the Hanseatic city of Lübeck.

Heinrich der Löwe förderte den um 1160 begonnenen, um 1220 vollendeten Bau des Ratzeburger Domes, der ein bedeutendes Frühwerk mittelalterlicher Backsteinbaukunst ist. Angesichts der angrenzenden Klostergebäude scheint die Zeit stehengeblieben zu sein.

Henry the Lion sponsored the building of Ratzeburg Cathedral, begun around 1160 and completed about 1220. It is a significant early example of mediaeval brick architecture. Considering the adjoining monastry building, time seems to have stood still.

Das von einem Wassergraben umgebene Ahrensburger Schloß wurde Ende des 16. Jahrhunderts gebaut und gilt als hervorragendstes Beispiel der Renaissance-Architektur. Mitte des 18. Jahrhunderts ließ ein Kaufmann das Innere umgestalten, wie es noch heute als Museum erhalten ist.

Ahrensburg Castle surrounded by a moat was built at the end of the 16th century and is known to be the most excellent example of Renaissance architecture. A merchant had the interior altered in the middle of the 18th century. Today is has been preserved as a museum.

Die fischreichen Seen- und Flußlandschaften der „Holsteinischen Schweiz"
lassen auch noch begrenzt eine berufsmäßige Fischerei zu, wie hier auf der
Schwentine zwischen Plön und Preetz – sehr zum Verdruß einer nahen
Kormoran-Kolonie (oder umgekehrt).

The lake and river areas of Holstein Switzerland abounding in fish only permit
a limited amount of occupational fishing, as is the case here on the Schwentine
between Plön and Preetz – very much to the annoyance of a nearby cormorant
colony (or the other way round?)

An Stelle einer alten Burg ließen die Fürstbischöfe von Lübeck am Großen Eutiner See ein barockes Schloß bauen. Auf der Freilichbühne im Schloßpark finden seit 1951 im Juli/August die „Eutiner Sommerspiele" zu Ehren des Komponisten Carl Maria v. Weber statt.

On the site of an old stronghold the prince bishops of Lübeck had a Baroque castle built at great Lake Eutin. On the open-air stage in the castle every July/August since 1951 the Eutin summer festival takes place in honour of the composer Carl Maria v. Weber.

Wahrzeichen Plöns im Herzen der „Holsteinischen Schweiz" ist das auf einem Berg liegende im Stil der Spätrenaissance gebaute Schloß (heute Internat). Mit den umliegenden Seen bietet das Heilbad ideale Reviere für Angler, Segler, Kanuten und Ruderer.

Plön's landmark in the heart of "Holstein Switzerland" is the castle (today a boarding school), on a hill and built in the style of the late Renaissance. The health resort with its surrounding lakes is ideal for angling, sailing, canoeing and rowing.

Die sechs mittelalterlichen Salzspeicher an der Obertrave in Lübeck waren zur Lagerung des wertvollen Salzes bestimmt, das Flußschiffe aus Lüneburg brachten, bevor es auf die seegehenden Hansekoggen verladen und über die Ostsee transportiert wurde.

The six mediaeval salt warehouses on the Upper Trave in Lübeck were meant for the storing of valuable salt which barges brought from Lüneburg before it was loaded on the seagoing Hanseatic vessels and transported across the Baltic.

Das Holstentor und die Türme der gotischen Kirchen bestimmen das Lübecker Stadtbild im Westen und dokumentieren die Macht und den Reichtum der einstigen „Königin der Hanse". Die UNESCO hat die historische Lübecker Altstadt zum „Weltkulturerbe" erklärt.

The 'Holsten Gate' (Holstentor) and the towers of the Gothic churches determine the townscape of Lübeck in the West and are proof of the power and riches of the form 'Queen of the Hanse' UNESCO has declared the historical old city of Lübeck to be a 'cultural heritage of the world.'

Seit 1913 kann man in diesem schönen Jugendstilgebäude Roulette und Baccara spielen: das Spielcasino von Lübeck-Travemünde steht als Symbol eines vormals mondänen Ostseebades, das Thomas Mann schon 1901 in seinem Roman „Buddenbrooks" liebevoll beschrieb.

Since 1913 roulette and baccara can be played in this beautiful Jugendstil building; the casino of Lübeck-Travemünde stands as the symbol of a onetime elegant Baltic resort which Thomas Mann so affectionately described in his novel "Buddenbrooks" in 1901.

Zwischen Travemünde und Niendorf gelegen bietet das sechs km lange, rund 15 bis 20 m hohe Brodtner Steilufer einen drastischen Kontrast zu der sonst weichen Küstenlinie der Ostsee in der Lübecker Bucht. Jährlich holt sich das Meer ein Stück Uferstreifen.

Between Travemünde and Niendorf the steep Brodten coastline offers a dramatic contrast to the otherwise gentle Baltic coastline in the Bay of Lübeck. Every year the sea carries off a piece of the bank.

So wie hier am Timmendorfer Strand sieht es überall entlang der Lübecker Bucht aus. Aber mit dem Ambiente im Hintergrund unterscheidet man sich voneinander: mit über 100 Hotels und zwei Golfplätzen gilt das Bad als exklusiver Vorort Hamburgs.

As here on Timmendorf Beach it looks the same all along the Bay of Lübeck. But with this ambience in the background there is a difference: with over 100 hotels and two golf courses the resort is an exclusive suburb of Hamburg.

Der Pagodenspeicher am Neustädter Hafen stammt aus dem Jahre 1830. Mit seinem getreppten Walmdach diente er zum Trocknen von Getreide. Die 750 Jahre alte Stadt veranstaltet alle drei Jahre (1990 usw.) eine europäische Volkstums- und Trachtenwoche.

The pagoda warehouse at Neustadt Harbour stems from the year 1830. With its stairlike hiproof it was used for drying grain. The 750 year-old town organizes an European folklore and national costume week every three years (1990 etc.)

Von Burgstaaken, dem urigen Hafen an Fehmarns Südküste, fahren nicht nur die Fischer auf die Ostsee, auch Hochsee-Angelkutter und Ausflugsdampfer (bis nach Dänemark) vermitteln binnenländischen Sehleuten einen Hauch vom großen weiten Meer.

Not only the fishermen sail to the Baltic from Burgstaaken, the quaint harbour on the southern coast of Fehmarn, also deep-sea fishing boats and excursion steamers (as far as Denmark) give inland sailors a breath of the great wide sea.

Seit 1963 verbindet die knapp einen Kilometer lange Schienen- und Straßen-brücke über den Fehmarnsund die Insel mit „Europa", wie die Fehmeraner sagen. Die hier verlaufende „Vogelfluglinie" ist die kürzeste Verbindung zwischen Skandinavien und Mitteleuropa.

Since 1963 the scarcely 1 km long rail- and road bridge over Fehmarn Sund connects the island to 'Europe' as the people of Fehmarn say. Travelling as the crow flies is the shortest connection between Scandinavia and Central Europe.

Das Herrenhaus Panker mit seinen zwei Flügeltürmen wurde um 1650 gebaut. Der französische Garten mit den italienischen Sandsteinfiguren entstand erst 1962. Heute gehört das 1760 ha große Gut mit einer berühmten Trakehner-Pferdezucht dem kurhessischen Hause.

Panker manor with its two wing-towers was built about 1650. The French garden with Italian sandstone figures came into being in 1962. Today the estate, 1,760 hectares in size with a famous 'Trakehn' breed of horses belongs to the House of Kurhessen.

Der Blick über die ostholsteinische Hügellandschaft reicht bis zur Ostsee. Im April/Mai blüht der Raps, eine aus Südeuropa stammende Kohlart, leuchtend gelb. Nach der Ernte werden seine braunen Samenkörner zu Speiseöl und Futtermittel verarbeitet.

The view over Eastern Holstein's hilly countryside reaches as far as the Baltic. The rape blooms in April/May – a type of cabbage stemming from Southern Europe, bright yellow. After the harvest the brown seed is processed for edible oil and fodder.

Das Schleswig-Holsteinische Freiluftmuseum in Molfsee (bei Kiel) beherbergt rund 70 alte Gehöfte, Scheunen und Handwerkerbauten aus dem ganzen Land. In etlichen wird auch heute noch gearbeitet, so wie „früher": Müller, Weber, Drechsler, Korbflechter …

The Schleswig-Holstein open-air museum in Molfsee (near Kiel) has about 70 old farmsteads, barns and craftsmen's buildings from the whole countryside. In some, people work today as in 'former times': millers, weavers, turners, basket makers …

Seit über 100 Jahren gibt es die „Kieler Woche", das größte deutsche Segelsportereignis. Bei den Wettfahrten auf der Außen-Förde treffen sich jedes Jahr in der zweiten Junihälfte über 1000 Boote aller Regatta-Klassen zum Kampf mit Wind und Wellen.

The largest German sailing event, 'Kiel week' has been in existence for over 100 years. Every year during the second half of June over 1000 boats in all regatta classes come together for the races on the Outer Fjord in a struggle with wind and waves.

Wahrscheinlich hat der Ritter Reinhold hier im 11. Jahrhundert seine „Reinoldsburg" (Rendsburg) auf einer Insel in der Eider gebaut. Um diesen Flußübergang auf dem alten Nord–Süd verlaufenden Ochsenweg haben Schauenburger Grafen und dänische Könige lange gekämpft.

Probably Knight Reinold built his 'Reinold's fortress' (Rendsburg) in the 11th century on an island in the Eider. Schauenburg counts and Danish kings fought for a long time for this river crossing on the old Oxen Path running North–South.

Ob Winter, ob Sommer: die goldgelb geräucherten „Kieler Sprotten" kamen schon immer – in der Ostsee gefangen und vor Ort geräuchert – aus dem fast 700 Jahre alten Eckernförde. In dem Ostseebad mit dem vier km langen Sandstrand braucht niemand Kurtaxe zu bezahlen.

Winter or summer, the golden yellow smoked 'Kiel sprats' – caught in the Baltic and smoked on the spot – always came from almost 700 year-old Eckernförde. In the Baltic resort with its 4 km long sandy beach visitor's tax is not levied.

Arnis, mit 500 Einwohnern Deutschlands kleinste Stadt, besteht praktisch nur aus einer 600 m langen Hauptstraße. 1667 verließen 62 Familien Kappeln, weil sie nicht leibeigen werden wollten und gründeten auf einer ehemaligen Insel in der Schlei ihre Siedlung.

Arnis, with a population of 500 is Germany's smallest town; it consists practically of one 600 metre long main street. In 1667 62 families left Kappeln as they did not want to become serfs and founded their settlement on a former island in the Schlei.

Der aus dem 12. Jahrhundert stammende, alles überragende gotische Dom ist das Wahrzeichen von Schleswig, der alten Handelsstadt an der Schlei; dabei nicht zu vergessen: Schloß Gottorf mit den Landesmuseen und Haithabu, das Handelszentrum der Wikingerzeit.

The Gothic cathedral from the 12th century rising high above everything is Schleswig's landmark, the old trading city on the Schlei; not to be forgotten: Gottorf castle with the district museums and Haithabu, the trading centre from Viking days.

Das um 1600 gebaute, den Reventlows gehörende barocke Herrenhaus Damp steht im Mittelpunkt einer ansehnlichen Gutshofanlage, zu der auch reetgedeckte Wirtschaftsgebäude aus dem 17./18. Jahrhundert, ein Armenstift, eine Kapelle und Katen für die Gutsarbeiter gehören.

Damp, the Baroque manor of the Reventlows built about 1600, is in the centre of a considerable estate which also includes thatched farm buildings from the 17th/18th centuries, an almshouse, a chapel and cottages belonging to the farm workers.

Eingebettet in das östliche Hügelland und umgeben von den vor 200 Jahren als Einfriedung ihrer Äcker entstandenen Knicks leben die Angeliter heute in ihren Reetdachhäusern ein beschauliches Leben. Vor 1500 Jahren hatten sie als Angelsachsen England „begründet".

Embedded in the hilly countryside of the East and surrounded by the quick-set hedges ('Knicks') caused by the enclosure of their fields 200 years ago the Angelites today live a contemplative life in their thatched houses. As Anglo-Saxons they 'founded' England 1,500 years ago.

Ob dänisch oder deutsch: beide Ufer der Flensburger Förde haben sich zu einem großen Wassersportrevier entwickelt; dennoch geht es überall ganz beschaulich zu. Von romantischen Sonnenuntergängen muß man nicht träumen, die gibt es hier nicht nur im Sommer.

Danish or German: both banks of Flensburg Fjord have become a great area for water sport: nevertheless, there is a contemplative mood everywhere. You do not have to dream of romantic sunsets, for they occur not only in summer here.

Das im 16. Jahrhundert für den Herzog von Schleswig-Holstein-Sonderburg im Stil der Spätrenaissance gebaute Glücksburger Schloß gilt als eine der schönsten deutschen Wasserburgen (heute Museum). Die Stadt Glücksburg ist das nördlichste Ostsee-Heilbad des Landes.

Glücksburg castle, built in the 16th century for the Duke of Schleswig-Holstein-Sonderburg in the style of the late Renaissance is said to be one of the most beautiful German water-surrounded castles (today a museum). The town of Glücksburg is the most northerly Baltic resort in the country.

Windmühlen, wie hier in Nübelfeld/Angeln, spielten im windumtosten Schleswig-Holstein seit jeher eine große Rolle. Wie schon bei der Bändigung des Wassers durch den Deichbau, haben auch beim Umgang mit dem Wind holländische Einwanderer Vorarbeit geleistet.

Windmills like this one in Nübelfels/Angeln have always played a great role in wind-swept Schleswig-Holstein. As in the case in taming the waters by dyke-building, Dutch immigrants have been pioneers in coping with the wind.

Vom Hafen an der 30 km langen Flensburger Förde gingen schon Mitte des 18. Jahrhunderts „Butterschiffe" auf Fahrt nach Westindien und brachten das zurück, was Flensburg berühmt gemacht hat: den Rum. „Rum muß, Zucker kann, Wasser darf nicht" heißt hier das Grogrezept.

As early as the middle of the 18th century 'butter ships' went from the harbours at Flensburg Fjord, 30 km long, to the West Indies and brought back rum which has made Flensburg famous. The grog recipe here is: rum is a must, sugar a can and water not necessary.

Die kulturellen Zeugen vergangener Zeiten, wie die Kirchen von Keitum (Bild) oder Morsum aus dem 13. Jahrhundert, erhöhen den Reiz der mit 99 qkm größten deutschen Nordseeinsel Sylt, den jährlich viele Hunderttausende Besucher zu jeder Jahreszeit genießen.

Cultural witnesses of past ages such as the church at Keitum (in the picture) or Morsum from the 18th century add to the charm of Germany's largest North Sea island, Sylt (99 sq km). Every year visitors come at every season in their thousands to enjoy it.

Dünen, Heide, Watt und Sandstrand: alles auf engstem Raum am Ellenbogen auf Sylt, dem nördlichsten Punkt Deutschlands; bis zum südlichsten der Insel, bei Hörnum-Odde, sind es 40 km. Dazwischen liegt ein durch seine vielfältige Natur faszinierendes Eiland.

On Sylt's elbow (the most northerly spot in Germany) there is everything in close proximity: dunes, heath, mud flats and sandy beach; to the most southern part of the island – at Hörnum-Odde, it is 40 km. In between lies an island, fascinating on account of the variety of its natural beauty.

„Graue Stadt am Meer" hat Theodor Storm seine Stadt genannt, das mag für neblige Tage zutreffen, sonst aber herrscht ein buntes Treiben von Marsch- und Geestbauern, Schiffern und Touristen in der kulturellen und wirtschaftlichen „Hauptstadt" Nordfrieslands.

Theodor Storm called his town 'the grey town by the sea'. That may be true for misty days, but otherwise it is full of colourful activity: farmers from the marshes and geest (regions), bargemen and tourists in the cultural and economic 'capital' of Nordfriesland.

Von der Walfangtradition des 18. Jahrhunderts ist auf Föhr, der zweitgrößten der Nordfriesischen Insel noch einiges zu spüren, obwohl der heutige Wohlstand aus dem anmutigen Eiland selbst gezogen wird: der Landwirtschaft und dem noch ergiebigeren Fremdenverkehr.

On Föhr, the second largest North Fresian island there are still traces of the whale fishing tradition in the 18th century. Today's prosperity comes from the charming island itself: agriculture and a tourist' industry which is even more lucrative.

Habel ist mit vier ha Fläche die kleinste von zehn Halligen im Nordfriesischen Wattenmeer. Die nur 100 m breite, mit einer Warft versehene Insel entstand mit der Sturmflut von 1362, der „groten Mandränke", die auch das sagenumwobene Rungholt verschlang.

With an area of 4 hectares Habel is the smallest of 10 holms ('Hallige') in the North Fresian mud flats. The island, only 100 metres in width and on raised ground came into existence with the flood of 1362, the 'great drowning' ('grote Mandränke') which swallowed up Rungholt steeped in legend.

„Rüam Hart, kloar Kimmen – starkes Herz, klarer Blick" lautet der Wahlspruch der Helgoländer, deren Insel aus Buntsandstein jetzt 100 Jahre zu Deutschland gehört. Jährlich genießen über 500 000 Gäste klares Wasser, saubere Luft und den zollfreien Einkauf.

'Rüam Hart, kloar Kimmen': a stout heart, clear eyesight is the motto of the people of Heligoland whose island of coloured sandstone has belonged to Germany for the past 100 years. Yearly over 500,000 guests enjoy clear water, clean air and duty-free shopping.

Wenn die Eider zugefroren ist, machen auch die Krabbenfischer von Tönning, dem alten Umschlagplatz zwischen England und Haithabu, Winterpause. Sonst ist der Hafen Ausgangspunkt für Fahrten zum neuen Eidersperrwerk und zu den Seehundbänken im Wattenmeer.

When the Eider is frozen over the shrimp fishermen of Tönning, the old place of transhipment between England and Haithabu, have a winter's rest. The harbour besides is the starting point for trips to the near Eider dam and the seal banks in the mud flats.

Wo die „süßen" Wasser der Treene auf die „salzigen" der Eider treffen, bauten Holländer 1621 ihr „Klein-Amsterdam" mit Grachten, Kanälen und Renaissance-Giebelhäusern auf: Friedrichstadt. Die Grachten- und Treene-Fahrten sind ein besonderes Erlebnis.

Where the 'sweet' (fresh) waters of the Treene meet the 'salty' ones of the Eider the Dutch built their 'little Amsterdam' in 1621 with grachts, canals and Renaissance gabled houses: Friedrichstadt. The canal and Treene trips are a special experience.

Das Leuchtfeuer von Westerheversand auf der Halbinsel Eiderstedt weist aus 40 m Höhe den Schiffen den Weg durch den Heverstrom und das Wattenmeer. Vor der Automatisierung der Befeuerung wohnten in den beiden Häusern zwei „hohe" Beamte: die Leuchtturmwärter.

The beacon of Westerheversand on the Eiderstedt peninsula shows the ships the way through the 'Heverstrom' and the mud flats from a height of 40 metres. Before the light became automatic two 'high' officials lived in both houses: the lighthouse keepers.

Große Bauernhöfe, die Haubarge (Heuberge), sind charakteristisch für Eiderstedt. Eingewanderte Holländer entwickelten diesen Bautyp seit dem 16. Jahrhundert aus dem friesischen Vierkanthaus: Er vereinigt Scheune, Stall und Wohnhaus unter einem mächtigen Reetdach.

Large farms 'haystacks' are characteristic of Eiderstedt. Since the 16th century Dutch immigrants developed this kind of construction from the Fresian square house: barn, stable and living quarters are all together under one massive thatched roof.

Flach, grün und naß: die Köge; eingedeichte, langsam zu Festland anwachsende Strand- und Wattgebiete bestimmen in weiten Teilen Dithmarschens den Blick nach Westen. Das, was wie unberührte Natur aussieht, ist in Wirklichkeit eine moderne Kulturlandschaft.

Flat, green and wet: the polders; beach and mud flat areas, surrounded by dykes and slowly becoming part of the mainland determine the view to the west in large parts of Dithmarschen. What looks like unspoilt nature, is in reality a modern cultivated landscape.

Der immer eisfreie Büsumer Hafen dient Fisch- und Krabenkuttern, Sportbooten und Ausflugsdampfern – und der „grüne" Strand vielen Urlaubern – als Liegeplatz. Selbst die „Heuler", die elternlosen Seehund-Babies, fühlen sich hier in der Aufzuchtstation wohl.

Büsum harbour, always ice-free serves as a resting place for fishing and shrimp boats, for sport boats and excursion steamers. Its 'green' beach serves the same purpose for holidays makers. Even the 'howlers': the parentless baby seals feel at home in the breeding station.

Den Namen „Prinzeßhof" hat dieser im 16. Jahrhundert in Itzehoe als Adelshof errichtete Bau von Juliane Prinzessin von Hessen, die hier von 1810—1860 als Äbtissin des adligen Klosters residierte. Heute ist hier das Museum des Kreises Steinburg zu Hause.

This building constructed in the 16th century in Itzehoe as a noble residence has got its name 'Princess palace' from Princess Julianne of Hessen who resided there from 1810—1860 as abbess of the aristocratic convent. Today the museum of the district of Steinburg is here.

Die 1754/56 von Cai Dose erbaute Rellinger Kirche hat einen oktogonalen (achteckigen) Grundriß, dem nach Westen ein im Kern noch romanischer Turm angegliedert ist. Der spätbarocke Zentralbau faßt mit seinen umlaufenden Emporen und Logen 2 000 Menschen.

The church of Relling built by Cai Dose 1754/56 has an octagonal layout to which, towards the west, a basically Romanesque tower has been joined. The late Baroque central building with its galleries and boxes running right round can seat 2,000 people.

Die ersten Deiche, die die Wilstermarsch bei Sturmfluten oder Hochwasser vor der Überflutung durch die Elbe schützten, haben holländische Siedler im 12. und 13. Jahrhundert gebaut. Hier liegt auch mit 3,5 m unter NN die tiefste Bodenstelle der Bundesrepublik.

The first dykes which protected the Wilstermarsch from the floods or high water caused by the Elbe overflowing were built by Dutch settlers in the 12th and 13th centuries. Here is also the lowest piece of ground in the Federal Republic – 3,5 metres below sea level.

Daß Schleswig-Holstein nicht nur ein Land für den Sommerurlaub ist, sondern gerade auch im Winter besondere Naturschauspiele (und Fotomotive) bietet, braucht angesichts dieser Elblandschaft bei Glückstadt nicht besonders betont zu werden.

It does not require stressing that Schleswig-Holstein is not only a region which offers special natural scenes and photographic motifs for the summer vaccation, but especially in winter which can be seen in this landscape at the Elbe near Glückstadt.

Der Fotograf
Horst Wöbbeking
wurde am 9. November 1938 in Bremen geboren.
Er wuchs in Worpswede auf, wo er bei Hans Saebens eine Lehre als Fotograf
machte.
Seit 1968 ist er selbständig als Industrie- und Landschaftsfotograf.
Herausgeber mehrerer Bücher und Kalender. Für sein Buch „Worpswede –
Bilder einer Landschaft" erhielt er 1981 den Kodak-Fotobuchpreis.

Der Textautor
Horst Goetzmann
wurde 1935 in Pommern geboren.
Er siedelte 1946 mit der Familie nach Lübeck über, lernte Mechaniker
und machte sein Abitur. Das Studium der Germanistik, der Literatur- und
Sozialwissenschaften in Hamburg schloß sich an. Seit 1975 ist er Fernseh-
und Rundfunkredakteur, z. Z. ist er auch als freier Journalist und Autor tätig.
Er lebt in Stormarn.